Of Chaos & Clarity

RUBU YARI

ZORBA BOOKS

Published in India by Zorba Books, 2017

Website: www.zorbabooks.com
Email: info@zorbabooks.com

Copyright ©RubuYari

ISBN 978-93-86407-74-0

Zorba Books Pvt. Ltd.(opc)
Gurgaon, INDIA

Printed at Repro Knowledgecast Limited, Thane

For,

Mom and Dad
Rubu Mamu
Siddharth Prakash
Jamaal Jackson Rogers
Kanika Agarwal
Petenienou Yeisei
Rügotsono Iralu

My thoughts on Yari's poems

Vulnerably honest

    I have had the privilege of reading Rubu Yari's beautifully movin poem collection called, 'Of Chaos and Clarity.' It is written in tw sections and is a journey from one state of mind to the other. Howeve the sense of destination is missing in the second section because she still journeying towards it. It is moving because the poet is so hone with her dark moments, opening her world to us without any attempt t hide her disorders as she calls them, and letting us understand how th long and painful quest for equilibrium feels.

    I am probably not off the mark in suggesting that the poetr writing has been cathartic for Yari, and that is as it should be. She say *These words, locked within, silently pacing around, this cocooned heart, searching f an outlet...I release you, fare thee well, memories.*

    Here is a human being who has suffered, struggled, rejected th easy way out and clung to life, even if it had been an arduous inner an outer life. I salute her persistent courage, the beauty of her generou spirit and her amazing will to live and share the christian faith that ha sustained her.

    The poems hit you in the pit of your stomach where many wh questions form. The first and second poems, 'My heart' and 'Odd' d prepare us for a different poetic experience. By taking us and herse back to childhood and letting us see her as a little girl-child, the poe makes herself utterly vulnerable. Could this be the reason for man adult mental disorders? Things suffered in childhood not addresse finding their way back and demanding attention by way of 'Chaos'?

    The poet has suffered, and suffered deeply, of that there is n doubt. She writes of her heart which is a well that holds 'buckets c anguish.' She talks of not fitting in, because she is 'odd, never remotel en.' We all know how that feels. It's a good lesson in learning to celebrate variety.

'Bullies' is a powerful poem on school life – a period of life which most people usually remember with nostalgic joy, but which was nothing but a miserable prison of 12 years endured by the poet with little support. There is a human touch at the end of the poem where she says she has now learnt to 'make them take a sip of their own medicine.' From that beginning we travel with her through the poem-journeys such as 'A million deaths' and 'My disorders,' 'The Little girl,' 'Death' and 'Fighting Rage.'

I have died a million deaths, this fragile heart, every word strikes at me, she writes, and ends with, *naked I came and naked I will go* but the real ending is the line – *not until victory is mine to grasp.* It is beautiful-powerful, the strength of those who have found grace, the strength of the meek, and we are exulted when she gets the last word – she will not go not until she has managed to grasp her victory.

'Trust' is a beautiful poem and proffers hope.

Though the poems are moving and painfully honest and resigned, they are not negative.

'The little girl' is about a girl-child - *she died a miserable death.* This is one of the saddest poems I have read on the murder of a young girl and her sister's helplessness to do anything.

'Death', is a grim poem, very embracive of death, looking at it as release, not horrid ending. It hints at a mind assaulted by wrong images. Fighting Rage surprisingly ends triumphantly, and manages to inspire.

Part two is called Clarity.

The poem 'Falling deeper' appears to be about the poet breaking away from tradition, from things that bind her.

The next poem 'Love is,' is very short and teaches what love is.

'Soul and Fire': the determination in this poem is uplifting. With the poet, we go through all the low points and rejoice when we reach the high points as here.

'Shadow man': this is a beautiful love poem, brings out what the beloved really finds valuable in her betrothed.

'Be still': This is such a beautiful poem - *How often do you just sit, listen and observe? Do so. It nourishes the soul. Be still.*

'Be You': is a poem about the poet finding herself, the poet opening up and being braver, and learning to be more herself: *fear no longer grips me, I write what I feel, I paint what I want' these fingers, that were once caged with fears, now run free like wild stallions. Her message is clear: if you don't let fear shackle you, you will see miracles, magic and marvel.*

'I am (part II)' strikes me as a spiritual war.

'Seeking the divine': part warning, part truth about the fact that preachers are also flawed humans.

'Happiness': such a simple, sweet poem.

'Perfection': *What is perfection? I believe /is the audacity to be/ oneself.* Can poem or a thought be more perfect?

Reading this volume, I felt as though Yari had placed in my hands not her poems, but her heart. So much trust. It was an honour to hold your heart for those few hours, few days, few moments of reading these poems, Yari.

'To Yari, poetry is a pursuit in finding oneself,' it says on the back cket of the poetry volume. I certainly think she has achieved that goal the book, especially in the second part, Clarity, without which the ook would be very incomplete. The journey comes full circle with both arts complementing each other. Thank you Yari for trusting us as urneying partners.

asterine Kire,
uthor of *When the River Sleeps*
he Hindu Literature Award Winner 2016

Preface

Within these pages are poems that reveals a journey of constant struggle with my chaotic mind. On the verge of quitting life, I found poetry, or poetry found me.

It has been a therapeutic experience ever since pen and paper became my closest companions. The words which had been hushed to silence, had finally decided to write them and share it, in hopes that someone would find my poems as an encouragement to them.

Of Chaos & Clarity, reveals a transition of my mind and heart from chaotic episode to a serene and peaceful realisations which has ever since changed my life. It took a great deal of patience and perseverance I, at times, almost gave up but I thank the interventions of the divine that had played a great role in calming the storms inside my head and channeling it into something beautiful. I believe, one does not achieve clarity without the chaos.

I would like to extend my heartfelt gratitude to my friends Luna Semo Khengye, Pradipta Brahma, Mohit Dhiman and Ajay Sharma for investing their precious time on this book.

I would also like to thank Easterine Kire for her expert opinions and undying support.

My love and wishes goes to all those who are struggling within. I hope you overcome mountains and be victorious in the paths you choose.

- Rubu Yari

Poet's note:

These words,
locked within,
silently pacing
around
this cocooned heart
searching for an outlet.
Keys,
of which I hold,
time it is,
to set them free.
For these words
can no longer be concealed
"behind layers of veneer"
For they were written only
to soar above.
I release you.
Fare thee well,
memories.

Contents

Part I- Chaos

My heart

My heart,
a poisonous well.
Only pails of malice
you can now draw from here
water that will kill.
No, I wished it not this way
I wished to satiate you
slake your thirst.
But darts of poison
you aimed at me
cackling, while I suffered.

This well now sullied
no longer holds
the essence of love
but depths of death
waiting for you to haul from it
buckets only of anguish.
So you would know how it feels
when I waded into this abyss.

Odd

I'm odd
never remotely even.
I never forebode
but that's just
how set I am.
Can you ever make
an even odd?
Can you ever ask
odd to be even?
I'm odd
never remotely even.

A tiny flicker

I'm engulfed
by a sea
of dubiety,
like tidal waves
drowning
the struggling
little debris
in the midst
of the
sea.

a belief
so small
have I,
like a tiny
flicker of fire
amongst
the vast frosts
that envelope the woods.

Trust

all I am left is
trust
upon
the Unseen.
for
what is seen
has forgotten
to be
trustworthy.

A million deaths

I have died a million deaths
this fragile heart
every word strikes at me
piercing like venomous darts
"Have thine own way Lord"
but do not make me an ode of your tragic art
"Naked I came and naked I will go"
not until victory is mine to grasp.

Tears

Count,
tell me about
the many tears
you've shed;
that you are left with eyes
that only see sorrow.
not a drop more to spare
come rain, come storm;
to heave away all the pain
off your callous heart.

My disorders

What is it
going on in my head?
I do not understand nor does anyone
would it be the one who created,
the only one to comprehend it.
Bestowed with three disorders
one controlling my body tics
one directing my urges for things manifold
and yet another that commands my mercurial emotions
makes me wonder
how much is left of me?
I declare,
Nothing.

Bullies

School,
never was a place for joy.
school,
a den of tyrants
a hood of bullies.
a place built of absolute despair.
those lucky ones
get away with friends.
others, a lot like us,
graduate with war scars
toughened, broken hearts.

Teachers?
stand silent or
bully you more
with sticks, pinches and words.
Parents?
scoff at every word you utter
Tutt at your complaints
and send you right back to school
saying "toughen up!"

School,
a prison.
12 years full,
had them all.
they threw me about like a ball
shoving me around like a pile of rag.
I won't lie,
I still see bullies
but I now know how
to make them wither.
for now, I know
how to make them take
a sip of their own bitter medicine

The little girl

She died a miserable death.
She was 13,
must have been
around 14.
None I know would wish a death like hers.
She was young and had a heart of gold
I wish I could have saved her,
but then,
I was just 10.

I wish I could turn
back around in time
I would have murdered that man,
just the way he maimed her
in that narrow lane -
even worse,
I would have carved out his gut
salted it with pain, remorse and agony
and watched him suffer
till he breathed his last
then I would have sold
his soul to the reaper
I would have bought her back,
kissed her.

I pray for you little girl,
I pray with this
murky thing that is my heart.
earth is a place only to breathe, decay and die.
heaven is your home now
not a soul beautiful as yours have I found
for, you truly belong up there
between the cotton clouds
while I scribble these lines, with tears in my eyes

oh! you scoff and you laugh
at my silly, sentimental being
for you are up there and I'm down here
below, buried six feet under guilt.
you will never be forgotten
O, brave one, for your grit
and the heart you possessed.
dear little one,
I love you oh! so much
from the deepest depth of my unpatched heart.
death might have taken you
but you lie still here,
the testament of your bravery
still lives with your little sister,
you so dauntlessly saved from
a fate that could have been hers;
and in my memories.

(O Death, where is your sting?
O Hades, where is your victory?
1 Corinthians 15:55)

Death

Dear Lord,
my head is on the edge of losing all its senses,
it's reaching necrosis.
nothing seems to be of help,
not the wise words or
a book of self-help.
All I see are lifeless beings
gallivanting and dawdling around
with no life to count.
We live in a world of doom
with no sight of florescence
sickening and saccharine
everyone has a mask they are wearing
seems all good and neat
each in its own place, lies
men, women, frantic, running around
nooses hung around their necks.

Suspended, I,
caught between dusks
hoping, soon morning will arrive
except, all I see is darkness
bleakly inviting me to its embrace
I have waited long
and can no longer
for I see no hope.
Why spend my life living only to die?
dying every minute I live.
maybe end it now
maybe reach out for a rope
beautifully garland it around my neck
latching the other end to a tree
saying my last prayers-
say to my God

"my apologies abba, I failed you"
after a brief moment of
dangling in the air
feel the air between my arms
like I always dreamed I would fly,
with my feet twirling in the air
zooming past through the blue skies
and wind whipping through my hair
but with no wind in my lungs
all calm, all dim.
Death.

Fighting rage

My dear rage, why do you hold on to me?
every time I resolve to depart from you
you come right back as if you loved me dearly
even when I succeed
for the briefest moment
heightened ease from the unceasing torment
assuming it's all over
I realize,
freedom is only for a little while
when you visit me a second time
wreaking havoc on all that I have built until then
watching me crumble until I kowtow.

Once again, I'm sitting in the porch
staring at the distance I had once covered
now I'm back to where it began
with rage setting my heart aflame
feeling guilty and pained
for all the struggles I have gone through
what then have I gained?
rage is a spark
that sets forth a wildfire
incinerating you inside out
smoldering away all sweet memories
replacing them with harsh realities
my dear, do not brood over your bitter past
bitterness of past is the very spark
that ignites a fire
you are hated, despised and condemned
you are only left with yourself and your own life to end
rage, how you love to watch me crumble
on my knees
kneeling before you, ever so humble.

Dear rage, hear this
you are not my God
my God, is almighty
He will deliver me from the clutches of your fury hands
lurking in my mind and heart
He will burn you and blow you away like fleeting chaff
for it is written-
"Smoke rose from his nostrils;
Consuming fire came from his mouth,
Burning coals blazed out of it.
He parted heavens and came down;
Dark clouds were under his feet.
He mounted the cherubim and flew'
He soared on the wings of the wind.
He made darkness his covering."
dear rage, I bid you adieu
for you know that the fire greater than you
has taken His seat in my heart.

Depression

Tears raining
lacking reasons
dark clouds above my head
shoulders droop
heart sinks
fearful of words
fear cutting in deep
curled up with my arms around my knees
weeping, the only release.

While the world moves in its own pace
the bed I lie becomes my own
little fort, a sanctum sanctorum
a second feels like an hour.
traumatizing waves of anxiety
gushing with vengeance towards me
I try to pull myself together
convincing that it is just another phase.
no, not to the psychiatrist I will go to
not the psychiatrist,
never the psychiatrist
but with every surge
every swell of perturbation
I feel a pull and a tug to the trenches below
I'm being buried underneath.
Slowly.
Surely.
Breathlessness.

I kneel and submit to prayers and meditation
but God seem to take his own time
I lean on medicines and sessions
but the doctor milk me of my money and my time.

I feast on medicines,
drugged away from reality.
neither God nor a doctor
neither prayer nor medicine
could set me off
this never ending downward spiral of anguish.

so, I lift up my pen to pen these thoughts
and string a poem
trying to draw out words
from my heart, mind and soul
because only the heart feels, only the mind knows
and the soul bears the brunt of it.
while I knit this poem word by word
my heart lightens and my mind is at peace
I thank God for making me, me
and I thank my doctor for saving another day
when I only wanted to end it
but most of all I thank thee, poetry
my healer, my therapy.
well, I guess while I wait on God
I might as well take my remedy.

Mute

My speech,
throttled by an invisible cork
hard it is to purge my feelings
you flare yours
in oratory declamation
belittling me
slowly killing
until,
my speech silence
and my voice mutes.

Part II- Clarity

Falling deeper

Forgive me
for I'm falling
into a world
unbeknownst to you.

I'm diving deeper
into the Universe
and beyond.

So much beauty.
So much power.
So much truth.

Love is

Love is not only what you do.
Love is what you have.
Then comes the 'do'.

Soul and fire

Deep down
within
this fatigued
soul,
a fire still burns.
Never
to
be
blown out,
I
shall
nurture it,
with tender
love and care.

Shadow man

You behave
like a shadow
that never leaves
me.
You cry, when I cry.
You laugh, when I laugh.
You dance, when I dance.
Like my shadow,

I love you.

Be still

How often
do you just
sit,
listen
and observe?
Do so.
I have.
It nourishes
the soul.

Be still.

Be YOU

Had always been afraid
of words and colours.
never felt qualified
for either.
But then,
I realize
these were my greatest assets
fear no longer grips me
I write what I feel
I paint what I want
I let words and colours
run through my fingers
while my heart
ushers them.
these fingers
that were once caged with fears
now run free like wild stallions;
a scrawled note or a messy canvas
it matters no more.

Dear you,
don't let fear shackle you.
The gifts bestowed on you
unleash them all and let it run wild
Then!
Only then will you see
miracles, magic and marvel
fear no more.
Just
be
YOU.

The night sky

I look upon the night sky
peppered as it is with dots and asterisks
even the thick veil of smog
couldn't hide its nonchalant splendor.

I lie in the grass, gazing at the silent heavens,
and I see it smiling back at me.
A retreat for the hopeless.
The night sky.

Love is Perfection

Peering through the thick veil of murky and soggy past
never calculated how long these memories would last
I hate to admit it
Life wasn't like a harmonious beat
but, a living hell,
trying to make ends meet.
surviving sometimes on gulps of air
I hungered for love and consolation
but was instead doomed to morbid desolation
I see men holding empty plates standing in staggering lines
waiting to receive the same
Where is love?
I wondered
Where is love?
a divine gift that has lost its worth
in this unfortunate world.
I sought for love all these years
never once realizing that-
I was Love
and I am Perfection
Are you seeking for love?
Come here, sit beside me
and
I'll show you love.

I am (part II)

I may be silent
but I can assure you
I will draw an arrow
without a glitch shoot it
right through your front lobe
and shatter your fragile ego.
but my war is not with you
or with bullets and darts.
I need only open my mouth
and proclaim what truth is.
It is in the tip of my tongue.

Can you face the truth?
I know, not, for sure.
see you at the battle front.
Come to me
armed to the teeth with barbs and bullets
I will come at you
the spirit of god on my right
and the living word on my left
while the holy father watches over me
with blessings of victory already at hand.

Come at me
bid your time
for you will need all your power and might
to wage a war against me
for I am the chosen one
and I bear the mark of the Holy One
etched on the gateway of my temple.
I am
(who I am.)

Nature Love

I would rather stay in the forest
and live among the dandelion fairies
who travel through the air.
the wind that blows,
the whispers of the mystical creatures
passing between tall bamboo grooves
filtering the wind, creating musical tunes
ringing in my ears gently.

Reindeers and wolves, owls and foxes,
crickets and frogs, fishes and dragonflies.

I lie down, while tall reeds surround me, protecting
as I watch the milky-way mesmerize me
with its countless stars
spread across its body.

Hold me mother nature,
don't let me go.
I don't want to leave,
not yet.

Seeking the divine

It is often at a sacrifice of a soul
does a preacher realize his mistakes and thrives.

One must.
So, at a certain point,
if they will,
learn to seek the divine alone,
and not from the lap of preachers
for, they too are broken souls,
just like us.

Love and humility

Love
transpires
humility.
If not,
it isn't true.

Happiness

a mug
of
black tea
wreathed
bread
a pen
a paper
and
a poem.
Happiness
is in

the simplest
of things.

Perfection

What is perfection?
I believe,
is the audacity to be
oneself.

Credits:

Credit for editing this book of poetry goes to
Luna Semo-Khengye and *Pradipta Brahma*

Book designed by
Mohit Dhiman

Illustrations by
Ajay Sharma

Ajay Sharma is an artist who works with Intermedia Installations and
Performance. He completed his Masters from Jamia Millia Islamia
University, New Delhi. He is the founder of the Syahghar Alternative
Photo Studio.
www.2bajaysharma.wordpress.com